SandCastle

Compound Words

# cat + fish = catfish

## Amanda Rondeau

Consulting Editor Monica Marx, M.A./Reading Specialist

ABDO
Publishing Company

Published by SandCastle™, an imprint of ABDO Publishing Company, 4940 Viking Drive, Edina, Minnesota 55435.

Printed in the United States.

Credits
Edited by: Pam Price
Curriculum Coordinator: Nancy Tuminelly
Cover and Interior Design and Production: Mighty Media
Photo Credits: BananaStock, Ltd., Corbis Images, EclectiCollections, Eyewire Images, Hemera, PhotoDisc, Stockbyte

Library of Congress Cataloging-in-Publication Data

Rondeau, Amanda, 1974-
    Cat + fish = catfish / Amanda Rondeau.
      p. cm. -- (Compound words)
    Includes index.
    Summary: Illustrations and easy-to-read text introduce compound words related to the seashore.
    ISBN 1-59197-432-1
    1. English language--Compound words--Juvenile literature. [1. English language--Compound words.] I. Title: Cat plus fish equals catfish. II. Title.

PE1175.R6655 2003
428.1--dc21

                                                                    2003048010

SandCastle™ books are created by a professional team of educators, reading specialists, and content developers around five essential components that include phonemic awareness, phonics, vocabulary, text comprehension, and fluency. All books are written, reviewed, and leveled for guided reading, early intervention reading, and Accelerated Reader® programs and designed for use in shared, guided, and independent reading and writing activities to support a balanced approach to literacy instruction.

## Let Us Know

After reading the book, SandCastle would like you to tell us your stories about reading. What is your favorite page? Was there something hard that you needed help with? Share the ups and downs of learning to read. We want to hear from you! To get posted on the ABDO Publishing Company Web site, send us e-mail at:

**sandcastle@abdopub.com**

**SandCastle Level: Transitional**

A compound word is two words joined together to make a new word.

# cat + fish =

# catfish

Matt and his uncle are fishing for catfish.

Matt likes to eat catfish for dinner!

# star + fish =

# starfish

Abby finds
a starfish.

She never saw
one before.

# sting + ray =

# stingray

A stingray is a wide, flat fish.

It lives in the ocean.

# sail + boat =

# sailboat

The Smith family likes the ocean. They sail their sailboat on the ocean.

# sea + shell =

# seashell

Sally and Liz find a seashell on the beach.

They wonder if a hermit crab is hiding inside it.

# gold + fish =

# goldfish

Bill named his goldfish Buddy.
He feeds the fish every day.

# Sue and the Giant Seashell

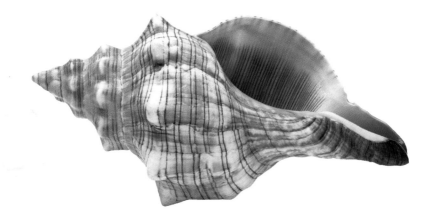

Sue fell into a giant seashell.

She floated over where the
stingray and catfish dwell.

A speedboat went by in a flash.

A sailboat glided by without
a splash.

Sue passed a water bug and a dragonfly.

She ended up at the lighthouse, safe and dry.

# More Compound Words

| | |
|---|---|
| beachfront | rowboat |
| bullfrog | seagull |
| cattail | seashore |
| drawbridge | seaweed |
| inland | swordfish |
| jellyfish | waterfront |
| lifeguard | waterproof |
| offshore | whirlpool |

# Glossary

**catfish**     a fish found in rivers and lakes that has tendrils around its mouth that look like whiskers

**dragonfly**   a large bug with a narrow body and two sets of wings

**dwell**       to live in a place

**lighthouse**  a tower near the sea that has a bright light on top to warn and guide boats

**sailboat**    a boat that is moved by the wind blowing against one or more sails

**seashell**    the hard covering of a sea animal like a clam

# About SandCastle™

A professional team of educators, reading specialists, and content developers created the SandCastle™ series to support young readers as they develop reading skills and strategies and increase their general knowledge. The SandCastle™ series has four levels that correspond to early literacy development in young children. The levels are provided to help teachers and parents select the appropriate books for young readers.

**Emerging Readers**
(no flags)

**Beginning Readers**
(1 flag)

**Transitional Readers**
(2 flags)

**Fluent Readers**
(3 flags)

These levels are meant only as a guide. All levels are subject to change.

To see a complete list of SandCastle™ books and other nonfiction titles from ABDO Publishing Company, visit www.abdopub.com or contact us at:

4940 Viking Drive, Edina, Minnesota 55435 • 1-800-800-1312 • fax: 1-952-831-1632